AF317007

# Myles Opens A Lemonade Stand

**Myles Brown**

Copyright © 2024 Myles Brown
All rights reserved
First Edition

PAGE PUBLISHING
Conneaut Lake, PA

First originally published by Page Publishing 2024

ISBN 978-1-6624-8316-5 (pbk)
ISBN 978-1-6624-8319-6 (digital)

Printed in the United States of America

*Myles Opens A Lemonade Stand* is dedicated to my grandmother Joyce Brown—an early childhood teacher—and my grandfather Joseph Brown, who was a businessman and dyslexic.

Special thanks to Thomas McBrien (my editor) and my mother and mentor, Megan Brown (coauthor).

It was the last week of the first grade when my mom found out that I would not be promoted to the second grade. I remember that day vividly. I had Kuk Sool Won class that evening. After class we stopped at my favorite restaurant in town. In fact, it was every six-year-old's favorite place in town. It was called Chick-fil-A. I had ordered a two-count Chick-n-Strips kid's meal with lemonade.

Mom was not very talkative the entire car ride. When we got home, I rushed to my room to finish my Lego castle. I heard the *bang, bang, bang* of cabinet doors slamming inside the kitchen. Then Mom yelled, "Myles." I ran into the kitchen, and she mumbled, "I had a long talk with your teacher and counselor today."

I started smiling, as my counselor always called me Myles the Smiles. I liked her a lot.

Then Mom said, "They think you would benefit from another year in the first grade."

The words left me speechless. I then whispered, "But Mom, all my friends are going to the second grade."

Mom replied, "Let's work on your reading this summer. I have asked Principal Sierra if you can return to school in the summer to retake the reading test."

My summer was now all about reading and writing. Mom had booked me into six weeks of both reading camp and creative writing camp at the University of St. Thomas. It was a beautiful place. Every Saturday I skipped along the tree-lined pathway to my class. It seemed to me that a lot of my friends who also struggled with reading and writing would enjoy it here. I thought it would be nice if they could all attend the summer program with me, but it didn't seem possible. Mom said it was super expensive; she was not even sure I could return next summer.

Over the summer, I was able to work on my phonics and fluency. When the camp ended, my reading teacher said I read very well. She seemed surprised when my mom told her that my school wanted me to repeat the first grade. However, it was at the creative writing camp that I learned why my teachers thought I would benefit from repeating the first grade. That's when I overheard the writing camp teacher whispering the words *developmental delay*. It was the last day of camp, and I had written a lovely fairy tale. My story was three pages long, but no one could read what I had written, not even me… My letters were written backward.

I read every book in sight that summer. I will never forget when my summer reading books arrived at my doorsteps. My mom ordered me some of the books that she had read when she was six years old. They were shipped from Australia, and they smelled and looked like they had been read many times before. The sight words at the back made it easy for me to read. I read *Play Time* and the *Our Friends from the Happy Venture* series, but my favorite book was from the *Olivia* books that I found at my neighborhood store. I came across the story *Olivia's Lemonade Stand*. When I finished reading the story, I could not stop thinking about the lemonade stand. I ran to my mom and blurted, "Mom, I want to open a lemonade stand!"

LEMONADE

My mom took a deep breath then asked, "How would you sell this lemonade?"

I replied, "Well, I have a lovely box that I can use to create my stand, I have the best recipe, and I can sell my lemonade right here outside of our home."

Mom thought for a moment and replied, "Let me think about this. You would need a location with lots of traffic and potential customers walking by…maybe outside of a grocery store or shopping center."

I started dreaming about my lemonade stand. What would it look like, who would come, and what would I do with the money? I thought about how helpful the summer reading and writing camps were, so I decided I would raise money to help other kids that struggled with reading or writing. I told my mom, and she thought it was a good plan.

"Social entrepreneurs are very special people, they start businesses to create positive changes in society."

My mom told everyone about my charity lemonade stand, and she even told my Cub Scout troop.

The scout leader asked, "What is the charity?"

I shouted, "Reading, a summer reading program."

My friend Addy's mom blurted, "There is an organization in Houston called Lemonade Day that encourages children to compete on Lemonade Day."

I got home and started my research.

I returned to school later that summer to meet with a reading specialist for my reading test. They said my reading level had jumped three levels! I received a lovely snack and was sent on my way. My mom called the school principal immediately.

The principal said, "I can tell he worked very hard over the past few months. His DRA score went up to 14, but we have determined that because he is only six, he will benefit from an additional year in the first grade."

Ym eman is Myles.
ym yrots is tuoba a ssecnirp
that sevil ni a eltsac
htiw reh mom and dad.
Reh name is Aivilo. Ssecnirp
Aivillo has 1 rehtorb. Yeht evil
in Acirfa in a tserof niar..

My mom was upset that I had to repeat the first grade. She kept mumbling, "You will change schools in September," but I was too excited about my lemonade business to think about September. I was looking forward to May 12—the annual Lemonade Day. Every week, I completed a financial literacy model. I even created a sketch of my stand.

That autumn, my mom was invited to a luncheon at Neuhaus Education Agency. She came home smiling and told me, "Myles, I found a charity for your Lemonade Stand. Neuhaus, they provide support to children and training to teachers to teach students with dyslexia."

That was when I found out that one in five elementary students struggle with reading. I said, "Bingo, that is my charity!"

I chose my mom as my mentor for my lemonade business. She was the best choice. My mom was once a manager at Coca-Cola; she knew everything about food and beverage. I called my mom my secret weapon.

In front of my new school was a lovely shopping center in an area called Sweetwater. There was a Kroger grocery store there, and every day on my way home from school, I would imagine myself selling bottles of lemonade there. I thought this was the perfect location for my lemonade stand. My mom agreed, and she suggested we ask the store if we could have my lemonade stand there instead of outside our home.

Aisle 17

Mom called Kroger, and we met with the store manager to discuss opening a lemonade stand.

He said, "Please contact the district office. I can only allow Cub Scouts at this time."

I thought, *But I am a Cub Scout.*

We emailed the district manager, who quickly responded, "Yes, we would love to host his lemonade stand!"

We returned to the store the next day and met with the store manager again to schedule the lemonade stand. They agreed to have it on Houston's Lemonade Day, May 12, from 10:00 a.m. to 2:00 p.m.

The week before the event, I found a carpenter to bring my sketch to life. I picked a rustic-red color for my stand. It was the same color as the Hawaiian lemonade I wanted to sell. My Hawaiian lemonade was made from fresh strawberries.

I planned my menu well. I would feature my special Hawaiian lemonade. I would also offer regular organic lemonade and diet lemonade. I had plastic cups to serve as well as ready-to-go small and large mason jars. I thought if I served my fresh, organic lemonade in mason jars, customers would be willing to pay as much as $5. My stand would also offer a few bottles of water, chips, and cookies.

LEMONADE
LEMONADE

Next, I started brainstorming a name for my stand. My mom called me the Juice King because I drank a lot of juice! When it was time to name my stand, that was the first name that came to mind: Juicy King. I challenged my friend Addy to compete with me on Lemonade Day to see who could sell the most lemonade, and we both registered on the Lemonade Day website. My stand would open at Kroger–Sweetwater while hers would be at another Kroger across town in Houston.

At last it was May and the last week of school. I made flyers for my lemonade stand and took them to class.

My teacher, Mrs. Hamill, turned to the students and said, "Myles wants to tell you about his lemonade stand."

I stood up and quickly passed my flyers out. I announced, "Tomorrow I am opening my lemonade stand at Kroger across the street. I will have Hawaiian lemonade, chips, and cookies."

Everyone was excited; they all wanted to stop by to try my special Hawaiian lemonade.

Tim asked, "Do you have a slogan?"

I responded quickly, "Yes! When life brings you lemons, make lemonade."

As I turned to sit down, Susan asked, "What is special about your lemonade stand?"

I smiled and replied, "My lemonade stand is important because it's for a charity that helps kids like me who can't sound out their letters or read what they write. I got help, and now everyone can read my writing. I can even read advanced chapter books. Ms. Hamill says that I will advance to the second grade next year!"

LEMONADE

May 12 soon arrived. Juicy King was open for business! I had freshly squeezed Hawaiian, regular, and diet lemonade. My sign read "Small $3 Large $5…$1 discount to Cub Scouts!"

My first customer was my cousin Kyira. She arrived in her stroller. I was not sure if she was more excited by my yellow balloons or my lemonade, but she was very excited!

29

One by one customers piled in. They were all interested in the charity. And just like I expected, they found fresh, organic lemonade served in a mason jar very appealing! I sold all my lemonade and packed up early. I called my friend Addy to see how she had done. She did well, but I had sold twice as much. Juicy King supported literacy, and I believe that made all the difference! Next year, I will compete with all the kids in Houston.

The End

# About the Author

Myles Brown is a philanthropist and entrepreneur. He is the CEO and founder of Juicy King. Myles started his lemonade business at age seven. He has operated his lemonade stand in the Houston area and donated a portion of his proceeds to help students with dyslexia. He has received several awards including Lemonade Day Houston Student of the Year, and at age twelve, he was named Lemonade Day Houston 2021 Entrepreneur of the Year.

Myles knows the importance of reading and commits all his business endeavors to help students succeed in the classroom. He was held behind in the first grade for having a low reading level. Determine to succeed, by the third grade, he read two levels above his grade. Myles will donate one book to an orphanage or school for every fifty books sold.

www.ingramcontent.com/pod-product-compliance
Lightning Source LLC
Chambersburg PA
CBRC090146150726
48196CB00019B/739